Cardinal Godfried Danneels

MESSENGERS OF JOY
How important is priesthood today?

GW00602613

Translated from French
by
Elena French

VERITAS

Published 1995 by
Veritas Publications
7-8 Lower Abbey Street
Dublin 1

Messagers de la Joie
First published 1990 by
Service de Presse de l'Archevêché
Wollemarkt 15
2800 Malines
Belgium

English translation copyright © Veritas Publications 1995

ISBN 1 85390 274 8

Scripture quotes are taken from the *Good News Bible* ©
American Bible Society, New York, 1966, 1971 and 4th edi-
tion 1976, published by the Bible Societies/HarperCollins,
with permission.

Cover design: Banahan McManus Ltd, Dublin
Printed in the Republic of Ireland by Paceprint Ltd, Dublin

Dear brothers and sisters,

This is an unusual letter: a bishop is writing to you about his priests, and on their behalf. And yet it should not come as a surprise: are priests not entrusted to you, as well? You too must be concerned with their holiness, their faithfulness, and their happiness. What do priests feel today? Who are they? What do they expect of you?

My purpose in writing is not to call attention to priests and bishops. We are not the greatest among you; according to Jesus himself, the greatest are the poor, the little ones. Nor do we wish to list our grievances, or beg for compassion; we certainly do not want to complain. But, with the author of the letter to the Hebrews, we dare to say, 'Remember your former leaders who spoke God's message to you' (Heb 13:7).

THE JOY OF THE APOSTLES

Before we speak of 'the daily burden and the midday heat' which we must bear and endure – as indeed must you – we should point out that there are many sources of joy in our lives.

The joy of our vocation
Young people often ask us, 'Why did you become a priest?' There is no short and simple answer. But something is alive within us, something which we cannot doubt or deny: our vocation. At some moment – perhaps suddenly, or perhaps after a long journey – each one of us has realised clearly, 'this is the direction I must take'.

Vocation came to us; we did not seek it or cause it to happen. We found it – stumbled upon it. And yet we have also chosen it freely: we have all said 'Yes' to this vocation. Were we in any way better than our peers, more talented, more perfect? Not at all. Were we different in some way? Apparently, yes.

How did this vocation manifest itself? We felt drawn to God and to those who were like us. Our hearts were somehow sensitive, attuned to the inner things in life, to invisible realities. This sensitivity emerged most clearly when we listened to the gospels; some sentences went straight to our hearts and we could not forget them. Every priest will tell you that he has his own favourite sentences which have stayed with him year after year.

Let me repeat that we have done nothing to deserve this call, and that we have done nothing to develop this sensitivity. It simply happened to be there, before we could do anything about it. Of course, we are very grateful to those who fostered and nourished it within us: parents, friends, teachers, people met by chance along the way. But we know beyond all doubt that this sensitivity, this vocation, did not come from them. It came from elsewhere, from Someone else. The Church recognised it as authentic and confirmed it through ordination. This gives us strength to keep on going, through the patches of fog and shadow.

A passionate love for Christ

There is something very special between us and Christ. He looked at us, and we followed him; he wounded us in the innermost depths of our souls, and we have never healed from this wound. We live in constant yearning for him. His words and his actions, his death and his resurrection are constantly before our eyes. The scriptures, the events of our daily lives – everything speaks to us of him.

This is why we are particularly drawn to the poor and the helpless, to the sick and the very young. In their cry, so often stifled, we hear the hidden voice of the poor

Christ, who lives in them. There are times when we resist, and our hearts grow hard; but we can find no rest until we have responded to this cry.

There are times when our sensitive hearts mislead us, and then people tell us: 'You are naive; you know nothing of the world. You speak a language which we do not understand, and you behave like maladjusted idealists.' There is little we can say in response, except perhaps that we are neither to be blamed nor to be praised, for there is nothing we can do about it.

We experience this passionate love for Christ with particular intensity when we celebrate the Eucharist, especially on Sundays. Even when the liturgy is poor, the surroundings tawdry, the congregation small, we are at Emmaus once again. Each time, we can once again give courage to those who suffer, saying to them, 'Was it not necessary for the Messiah to suffer these things and then to enter his glory?' (Lk 24:26). With the help of the scriptures, starting with Moses and going through all the prophets, we explain to them that Christ is in everything. Then we gather with them around the table, and we break the bread. And they return to the city to tell others about it (Lk 24:25). Of course, both the fervour and the radiance of the Eucharist are somewhat weakened by the fact that we have so much on our minds on Sundays. However, we rediscover all its glow in adoration, the interiorisation of the Mass, which prolongs the radiance of the Eucharist.

Giving life

In preaching, we bring words of life to men and women: a spring flows forth, and in the sacraments it becomes an abundant outpouring. We are not ourselves the source of this life. Christ is the one who baptises, who gives his body for us to eat, who grants forgiveness. However, it is true that he has no mouth, no voice, no hands, no feet but ours. We are channels and instruments.

The priest is not only a prophet; he is also a father. Ignatius of Antioch spoke of this as early as the year 100; he wrote that the bishop and the priest are 'the image of the Father'. The priest gives life, as a father does. The hereditary connotations of paternalism which are associated with this word can take nothing from the reality; every truth can be distorted. St Paul wrote: 'For even if you have ten thousand guardians in your Christian life, you have only one father. For in your life in union with Christ Jesus I have become your father by bringing the Good News to you' (1 Co 4:15). With all due modesty and proportion, we can follow in his footsteps and say the same.

A passionate love for the Church

Those who love Christ also have a passionate love for the Church; one cannot love the head without loving the members as well. Priests care about the Church, even when they suffer because of her. This does happen; for within the Church there is weakness, compromise, luke-warmness, complacency and sin. Yet, beneath these afflictions, she carries her mystery: she is the body of our Lord and the temple of the Holy Spirit. Priests tend to care more and more for the Church as they grow older. The same was true of St Paul, whose love, tenderness and compassion for the Church are greatest in his later letters, those he wrote from prison to the Ephesians, the Colossians and the Philippians. He speaks of the Church as the 'glorious' wife, 'pure and faultless, without spot or wrinkle or any other imperfection' (Ep 5:27).

Priests, too, sometimes criticise the Church, rightly or wrongly. But, each time, we realise that everything we have comes to us from the Church: the scriptures, the sacraments, the pastoral responsibility. She also gives us our brothers in the priesthood, the presbyterium which surrounds the bishop. And we have received all of you –

that portion of the people of God whom we may serve in the Lord – from her hands. Without the Church, we would be nothing.

Finally, our credibility comes to us entirely from the Church. It is because of the Church that children, the sick, the troubled, the poor and the unhappy, those in despair and those who are anxious, come to us. In ourselves, we are far too weak and sinful to warrant the trust which people have placed in us for centuries, and still continue to place in us. By ourselves, we could never enjoy such credibility, precisely because we do not deserve it.

Inner joy

Much of our joy is the inner joy of prayer and reflection. Even when prayer is difficult and dry, it is a fresh spring where we can quench our thirst after the heat of the day; it is a warm fire to guard us against the cold indifference that sometimes surrounds us.

In prayer, our hearts set aside their protective shells. When the stress of work threatens to stifle us, we find our rhythm once again by praising, thanking and glorifying God. Our hearts expand, becoming as wide as the ocean, as vast as the universe. This is especially true when we pray the Psalms. If we feel sad and disheartened, the day's psalm of praise in the Book of Hours reminds us that we must speak on behalf of millions of others who, on this particular day, are happy and joyful. Conversely, a lamentation or a psalm of petition, when prayed on a bright and happy day, makes us aware of those who suffer and are afflicted elsewhere in the world. Praying the Psalms broadens our vision to universal dimensions, preserving us from the capriciousness of passing moods.

There is yet another joy in our prayer: that of interceding for others. The intentions of all the members of our families and communities, the intentions of the entire world, pass through the hearts of priests and are placed before God. The priest is Moses, interceding on the mountain top while the Israelites battle. Moses needed Aaron and Hur to support his arms (see Ex 17:8-13); in the same way, you must help us to pray, for we are your intercessors.

The joy of gospel freedom

'Everyone who has left houses or brothers or sisters or father or mother or children or fields for my sake, will receive a hundred times more and will be given eternal life' (Mt 19:29). This passage challenges us in a special way. There is joy in renouncing good things and in becoming detached from them. In these times, when we so easily become attached to many things, it can be difficult to avoid egocentricity. We are often caught up in the whirlwind of daily existence. But we also know – and we know it from experience – that detachment can bring joy.

There is joy in giving up a big salary, comfort, and future security; there is joy in living a life of poverty and sobriety. Which one of us has not fallen under the spell of the 'Franciscan' passage in the gospels which speaks of the birds in the sky and the lilies in the field? However tentatively we may tread the path of boundless trust in the Heavenly Father, who 'knows that you need all these things' (Mt 6:32), we intuitively know that happiness must be sought – and is to be found – in this direction. The same applies to celibacy – but more about that later. As for obedience, so often portrayed as a strait-jacket which is inflicted upon us, it actually liberates us from personal preferences, and allows us to be more easily integrated into the powerful jet stream of God's plan for the Church, for humankind, and for the universe. Obedience does not weaken us; it greatly increases our strength, because through obedience, our strength is directly replenished by God's all-powerful will.

Finally, in those who are poor, chaste and obedient, every faculty is sharpened and refined. Their sight is clearer, their hearing sharper; they can hear from a greater distance, with less interference; they feel with greater intensity. There is no doubt that those who are more sensitive are also capable of greater suffering – those who have sensitive ears are more likely to be disturbed by dissonance and background noise; but they can also hear Mozart and Schubert, and that is something nobody would want to miss!

THE HEAVY BURDEN AND THE MIDDAY HEAT

It would hardly be honest to make no mention here of the difficulties we are experiencing these days. We have feelings and reactions, however much we may strive to control them and to integrate them into the perspective of faith.

Fewer and older
The number of priests is decreasing and their average age is increasing. There are fewer vocations (although the numbers are well above what public opinion generally assumes). Priests sometimes find themselves wondering whether their congregations will have priests when they are gone. The work-load increases with each passing day, and we are saddened by the fact that we cannot continue to do everything as thoroughly and conscientiously as we would like to.

We know very well that evangelisation is not merely a matter of numbers. It is not the first time in history that there have been 'few workers to bring in the harvest';

Jesus himself spoke of this. The world does not come to an end simply because one priest has to provide for the needs of several parishes; it has happened before in our own country, and it is happening in other parts of the world as well. But we know how good it is when a priest can live among his parishioners, on the same land, and be fully part of their joys and their sorrows. It is true that the disappearance of the priest who is exclusively attached to one parish can often produce an awakening of the laity and an enabling sense of co-responsibility. Experience has shown, however, that these very same lay people are the ones who then ask for priests; for without a priest, they soon lose their energy and their enthusiasm.

Building bridges between opposite shores

Today, many priests are still very close to their communities. They take part in many aspects of people's lives. They share in the joyful experiences of births, communions, confirmations, and weddings. They know the silent joy of experiencing the trust of so many people; the joy of being channels of reconciliation and forgiveness for those who come to them, sometimes from a great distance; the joy of contemplating the quiet holiness of so many ordinary people whose daily existence bears living witness to a deep faith, a great hope, a love that is as strong as it is discreet. However, priests must often pass from great joy to deep sadness within a few moments. This need to shift gears, to empathise alternately with joy and with sorrow, makes great demands of their hearts. It can be exhausting, but it also gives them a special serenity, a certain satisfaction, a gladness.

Pastoral work often means that we must stand in midstream, half-way between two shores. Every priest is familiar with the tension between justice and mercy, between doctrine and practice, between requirements and compassion; between what the great Church teaches and what is possible to the poor believer. Some people expect priests to be rigorously orthodox, adhering literally to every detail; others expect realism, a recognition of the need to adapt and of the need for 'inculturation'. Priests can be trapped between liberals and conservatives. Poor St Christopher, carrying the infant Jesus between two shores which want nothing to do with each other!

New and difficult issues

Priests today must deal with an ever-increasing number of new and difficult issues. These tend to be moral issues: problems linked to Aids, bioethics, the ethical implications of economic and political problems, marriage problems, the painful question of divorced people who remarry, the criteria for admission to the sacraments – and this is only the tip of the iceberg.

In the past, issues such as these never went beyond the expert's office or the moral theologian's desk. Today, they are discussed in every living room. Individuals often have to make decisions on very serious matters, alone. Who is there to help them? Priests are not experts; the formation they receive is a general one. And people often want a clear and immediate answer to their questions. Yet any single item on the evening news can raise so many questions that a whole assembly of learned scholars would not be able to resolve them all.

The impoverishment of Christian memory

These are complicated questions; and the task of answering them becomes more difficult when we realise that Christian memory, for many of our people, has become thin and threadbare. They have few Christian concepts left; they have no framework within which to integrate whatever answers we can give. They have lost their

Christian mother-tongue. This makes it twice as difficult and awkward to answer their questions in a way they can understand.

Priests encounter this problem every day. They struggle to translate lengthy gospel passages and Church texts into more accessible language. Sometimes their efforts are successful; but not always. This is not necessarily due to incompetence; quite often it is simply because they are faced with an impossible task. How can we transpose the reality of treasures of faith such as grace, redemption and resurrection into terms borrowed from the popular jargon of newspapers and television? An understanding of a shared mother-tongue is a prerequisite for communication.

Conversely, there are many terms and concepts which are familiar to everyone today – authority, democracy, co-responsibility, power, government – but which cannot be used in their ordinary sense when dealing with Revelation, with faith, with the Church. They can only serve as analogies. It is like taking a ready-made suit off a store hanger and saying, 'This will do,' only to discover, later, that the jacket is too small or too big. Before they can become part of Christian and Church language, these terms will have to be filtered, their meaning adjusted to the realities they are meant to express. For example, in the Church – unlike the rest of society – to govern is to serve, and those who exert power must make themselves the least of all.

We, as priests, must hold ourselves partly responsible for this twofold deficiency – ignorance and impoverishment of language. When I describe the problems which confront priests today, I am not trying to apportion blame; I am merely stating facts. Recently, a priest said to me, 'My time and energy are spent proclaiming, explaining, and proving things which should be obvious to every

Christian.' There is little point in complaining; but the fact is that a huge effort is needed in the area of catechesis and formation in faith. And the first priority is to re-learn a mother-tongue.

A treasure in earthen jars

Most of our suffering is caused by our own fragility, our own weakness. 'Yet we who have this spiritual treasure are like common clay pots [the priesthood].' (2 Co 4:7). St Paul spoke of 'a thorn in his flesh', and we each have our own thorn to endure. The apostle has not told us what the thorn was: perhaps it was an illness or handicap, or a chronic disease; perhaps moral suffering or weakness; perhaps the painful memory of his past persecution of the Church. We shall never know; and this is just as well, for as a result the image of the 'thorn in the flesh' is sufficiently imprecise to signify anything that can be an obstacle to any one of us in his apostolic work.

There will always be something, in every priest's life, from which he will insistently ask God to deliver him: 'Lord, take this from me! You too will benefit, if you do, for I shall be able to serve you more efficiently; I shall bear more fruit.' But God answers, 'My grace is all you need, for my power is greatest when you are weak' (2 Co 12:9). The suffering of every apostle – today as in the past – is never accidental; it is never an unimportant detail. It is essential, for it is the infallible means by which God can preserve the apostle from relying on his own strength. When St Paul barely avoided being lynched (for condemning the cult of Diana and for ruining, by his preaching, the goldsmith Demetrius' flourishing trade in images of the goddess) in the circus in Ephesus, he wrote, 'We want to remind you, brothers, of the trouble we had in the province of Asia. The burdens laid upon us were so great and so heavy that we gave up all hope of staying alive. We felt that the death sentence had been passed on us. But this happened so that we should rely, not on ourselves, but only on God, who raises the dead' (2 Co 1:8-9).

Why am I telling you all these things? It is not from any desire to complain, or to make a big show of our sufferings; it is simply because we are your priests and we want to open our hearts to you. With St Paul, we say: 'God knows us completely, and I hope that in your hearts you know me as well.... We have spoken frankly to you.... I speak now as though you were my children' (2 Co 5:11; 6:11.13).

WHAT IS A PRIEST?

It is even more important for us to tell you who we are than for us to share our burdens and our joys with you. What is a priest?

To be is more important than to do

A great deal has been said and written about priests in recent years. There are even 'divergent' views of priesthood. Many have tried to provide definitions based on their own particular perspectives. Sociologists have explored the place and role of priests in society, and have attempted to explain how they can be more effective. Psychologists are interested in what priests feel; they ask questions about priests' subjective environment, their motivations and their emotional problems.

How can we define a priest? People often want to define priests on the basis of what they do; they assume that activities determine identity. There is some truth in this, of course; but this approach does not look beyond the surface, and does not reach deeply into the reality of priesthood. Moreover, many of the things priests do can in theory be done by others. In times of shortage, others – male and female religious, deacons, pastoral leaders, lay volunteers – have, in fact, taken on some of the tasks associated with priesthood – and it is fortunate that they have. If we were to define priests on the basis of what they do, excluding those activities which others may, if necessary, perform in their place, only a few functions would remain: the Eucharist and the Sacrament of Reconciliation – which, however, are essential to the community.

This definition reduces the priest to a skeleton. We cannot define him exclusively in terms of what he alone can do. Take, as an analogy, the difference between men and women: if we were to consider each sex exclusively in terms of its specific biological properties, the richness of each would be greatly reduced. Men and women often do the same things, but they do them differently. The same is true of priests: whatever they do, they do as priests – differently.

We must therefore define priests in terms of what they are. This cannot be understood outside the context of faith. The priest's being is invisible. To understand a priest, we must look at him in terms of God, of Christ, and of the Church.

In the person of Christ, head of the Church

The source and the roots of priesthood are in Christ; it is he who calls us and sends us. The priest is the *apostolos* – the one who is sent by Christ. We might say, however, that all believers are called and sent. Wherein lies the distinction?

The priest is called and sent on a mission that is unique and specific: to make Christ present in his Church, as her head, as the One who saves and sanctifies. Christ is the whole body, the head and the members. Thus, priests are members of Christ, with the other faithful; but as the ones who represent Christ-as-the-head, and make him present, they are also members of Christ *for* the faithful, and face-to-face *with* the faithful. Priests are taken from amongst human beings, but they are placed in their function for human beings, in order to work for them *and* amongst them. The head is not separate from the members, yet it is not identical with them. In the same way, priests, despite their profound solidarity with the faithful, remain other. While they belong to the people, they also stand face-to-face with them.

Participation in the unique priesthood of Christ therefore takes place on two planes: all the faithful participate through the baptismal priesthood; priests also participate through the ministerial priesthood which they receive at ordination. The two modes do not coincide: they differ in nature, not in degree; they are not interchangeable, and neither one can be reduced to the other. However, they cannot be separated, for the priesthood of the priest is entirely directed towards that of the faithful. It is by nature a means. The priest exists for the faithful. The priest's priesthood exists for one purpose only: to make possible the priesthood of the people, to enable the faithful to make their whole being and their every action a spiritual offering to God.

Thus, it would benefit no one if the two priesthoods were to be confused, or if the dividing line between the two were to become less clearly defined, or if they were to be set in artificial opposition to each other. On the contrary, we would all be enriched if priests became more fully priests and lay people more fully lay. The full presence of Christ among us – as the head of his one body, and as its members – is at stake.

The same reality can be expressed in another way. The priest carries within himself a special presence of Christ, and he is invested with the Spirit in a unique way. This does not make him invulnerable to weakness, ignorance or error, nor even to sin. All his actions are not equally guaranteed. His sacramental acts are fully guaranteed: a sin committed by a priest can never invalidate a sacrament. However, many of his other actions may be marked – even deeply scarred – by his human inadequacies and by sin. It is therefore his duty to strive continuously for conversion, to seek – through study, meditation and experience – the grace to discern what 'builds up' the community and what 'pulls it down' (see 2 Co 10:8). To this end, he must pray, and he must allow himself to be helped, corrected and supported by his brothers and sisters, priests and lay people, and by the Church. He must also be mindful of the saints who have gone before him, and of all that they did.

In the name of the Church
The priest does not only stand face-to-face with the Church community; he also stands within it. He prays, and he offers the Eucharistic gifts to God, in the Church and in its name.

This does not mean that the community delegates the priest to pray and to offer sacrifice. Indeed, the community's prayers and sacrifice are entirely assumed in the one prayer of Christ and in his gift of his own self. The gifts and prayers of the Church coincide completely with those of its head; nothing is added. It is precisely because the priest represents Christ as the head that he can also act in the name of the members, in the name of the Church.

The essential presence of the ministerial priesthood within the Church has a further significance. The priest makes visible the deepest essence of the Church. Her essence does not spring from herself; she receives herself entirely from Christ. The Church does not exist by her own grace; her strength does not come from herself. All that she is, all that she does, she receives from Christ and from his Spirit, through the channel of the ministerial priesthood of the bishops and priests.

The priest is given to the community from elsewhere. It is true that a community may propose a candidate, but the community cannot ordain him nor give him a mission. The Christian community cannot found itself, or build itself, or maintain itself: it receives itself from elsewhere. The ministerial priesthood both signifies and guarantees this.

None of this lowers the status of the laity, or places lay people under tutelage. On the contrary, it provides the very foundation of their identity and of their mission. Priests and lay people are not rivals; they are complementary and inseparable. Under certain circumstances, of course, lay people can and must assume tasks which are normally the province of priests. This is not without precedent in the Church. But even in such cases, lay people do not in fact replace priests; when the priest is absent, his chair remains empty. We cannot think in terms of rivalry or of replacement, but rather in terms of inclusion.

In practice, we often encounter difficulties in expressing these realities. In Corinth, St Paul had to deal with the problem of establishing order and harmony among a large number of different and divergent charisms. Today we are faced with the problem of articulating and ordering the dual priesthood within the Church. It might be helpful to re-read 1 Corinthians, chapters 12 and 14, for the solution is the same today as it was then. St Paul's conclusion is clear and emphatic: 'God does not want us to be in disorder but in harmony and peace' (1 Co 14:33).

A single priesthood – multiple theologies of priesthood
More than one attempt has been made to provide a theological synthesis of the ministerial priesthood. This is not because the nature of this priesthood is unclear; it is rather because the reality of the priesthood is so rich that it cannot be expressed in one attempt, in one theology. No single theological perspective can embrace this reality as a whole.

Some theologians look at priests primarily in terms of their service to the Word. This involves much more than preaching homilies. Sacraments, too, are words – powerful, definitive and fully effective words; indeed, their power is so great that they are independent of the inadequacies or the moral mediocrity of the person who speaks them. Sacraments are concentrated and super-effective words. And it is through the Word that the priest gathers his community and holds it together – especially through the supreme form of the Word: the Eucharist, sacrament of unity. The concept of the priest as servant of the Word – in its broadest sense – is a legitimate theological approach to priesthood.

Other theologians approach the priesthood in terms of the priest's Eucharistic service. Indeed, the priest's primary role is to make the Paschal sacrifice of Christ present within the community. And this automatically implies another service: the proclamation and preaching of the Word, which must result in an awakening of faith, and thus lead to the Eucharist. This in turn implies a further service: through the Eucharist, the priest founds and builds the community; he nourishes and unifies it.

For others, the priest is first and foremost the builder and guarantor of unity. He is the shepherd who, by the strength of Christ's Spirit, gathers the flock. To this end, he has two means at his disposal: homilies and sacraments.

Finally, there are those for whom the priest is the man of mystery, of communion, and of mission. In a secularised world, the priest, through his ordination and his function, is witness to mystery. His identity is a matter of faith. He bears witness to the good news of God's grace; he is a minister of the mysteries. In a divided world, he is the servant of communion. He takes his place in the crown of priests around the bishop; he is the guarantor of unity and cohesion within the community, in faith and in charity. In a world where many know nothing of Christ, the priest walks among the people – together with the other ministers, with the lay people and with the bishops – as a man of mission who takes charge of the Church for the salvation of the world.

No theology of priesthood is entirely satisfactory. Each one omits something of the integral richness of priesthood. Priesthood can only be fully understood in the light of faith, and faith is always much more than any single theological synthesis.

Preacher, celebrant and pastor

One thread, however, runs through all of these theological approaches: in all of them, the priest makes it possible for Christ himself to continue speaking to, sanctifying and leading his people in his Church, in an audible and visible way, as a good shepherd. Through the priest, Christ continues to visit his people, by means of the gospels, the sacraments and pastoral charity, 'until he comes again.'

Preaching is more than eloquence

The priest proclaims the Word on behalf of Christ. But does not every believer do the same? Was the proclamation of the gospel not entrusted to all, at the first Pentecost? Are not all those who received the Holy Spirit prophets? (See Ac 2:17-18.)

Indeed, the priest is not the only one who proclaims the Word. It is quite possible that, from a technical standpoint, others can do it better, with greater conviction and passion. There are lay people who have a remarkable knowledge of theology, and who have received an excellent formation; some are better speakers than many priests, and are more gifted in communication; some are better at knowing and relating to their audiences. Ordination does not confer or guarantee these talents and skills, although the Church would think twice before ordaining someone who did not possess them to some extent. However, the specificity of priestly preaching lies elsewhere.

The priest has a particular charism. His preaching is guaranteed, at least when it echoes the preaching of the whole Church. He carries within himself the guarantee that his preaching is 'apostolic' – that is to say, that his words go back authentically to Christ and to the apostles. Christ himself speaks the priest's words to his people, here and now, and they carry his full authority. This is true even of the clumsiest of speakers. Even if his words have no emotional impact; even if he is a failure as a speaker; even if his choice of words is not as good as it might be – yet his word is the word of Christ and remains the word of Christ. It can never be replaced. A poor, untalented preacher might say, with St Paul, 'When I came to you, my brothers, to preach God's secret truth, I did not use big words and great learning. For while I was with you, I made up my mind to forget everything except Jesus Christ and especially his death on the cross. So when I came to you, I was weak and trembled all over with fear, and my teaching and message were not delivered with skilful words of human wisdom, but with convincing proof of the power of God's Spirit. Your faith, then, does not rest on human wisdom but on God's power' (1 Co

2:1-5); and again, 'And there is another reason why we always give thanks to God. When we brought you God's message, you heard and accepted it not as man's message but as God's message, which indeed it is' (1 Th 2:13).

A celebrant is not just an animator
Priests celebrate the Eucharist and the other sacraments. Even if they do this with great care, sacraments are always discreet and unspectacular events - poor events, in other words. The rituals are sparse and brief. They have little or no tangible effect; certainly, they have no physical effect (the Eucharist does not satisfy hunger, and baptism does not wash the body). Nor do they have any psychological effect; the ritual often has no emotional resonance, and sacraments can be administered and received almost coldly. Their effect lies elsewhere. Their power has a different source: it springs from the paschal mystery of Christ, a mystery that is made present by the ritual. The priest traces the ritual circle within which Christ manifests himself, in sovereign freedom, because he is faithful to his promise. Nevertheless, even when he is not a gifted animator, the priest has a duty to make continual efforts in this area as well.

A pastor is more than a leader
Priests are also pastors. Once again, this is not a service they perform as a result of any particular human skills and talents. We could easily think of other people who have a greater gift for leading, accompanying, gathering and motivating groups of people; others who are better equipped to deal with tensions and conflicts. But let me repeat that what is specific to the priest's pastoral mission does not reside in these gifts. His 'authority' does not come to him from himself; it comes to him from Christ. 'Whoever listens to you listens to me; whoever

rejects you rejects me; and whoever rejects me rejects the one who sent me' (Lk 10:16). We are made aware of this whenever we read St Paul; he is very conscious of the fact that it is by Christ's authority that he leads the community.

Is there not a great danger in this? Temptations such as pride and the desire to dominate may lie in wait for the pastor around any corner. And how are we to reconcile all of this with the growing 'democratic reflex' of our modern societies? Priests cannot ignore the Bible's many warnings against 'bad shepherds who think only of their own needs', and against 'mercenaries who do not love their sheep'. The scriptures are there to alert us to these dangers. The members of our congregations must also take it upon themselves to remind priests of their duty to be humble and available. Finally, the suffering that is always present in any position of leadership and responsibility, especially in our time, inevitably brings humility.

Only through the eyes of faith can we see priests for what they really are: men of God, whatever their deficiencies, their faults, their sins. Simple, ordinary people are often the first to understand this. They have a spontaneous knowledge, a pre-logical intuition of what priests are. Francis of Assisi, for example, said: 'God gave me such great faith in priests who live according to the laws of the holy Church of Rome, because of their ordination, that if they persecuted me, I should still turn to them for aid. And if I were as wise as Solomon and met the poorest priests of the world, I would refuse to preach in their parishes against their will. I am determined to reverence, love and honour these priests, and all others, as my superiors' (The Testament of St Francis). It was a simple woman of Shunem who immediately recognised in Elisha 'a holy man of God', and said to her husband: 'Let's build a small room on the roof, put a bed, a table, a chair and a lamp in it, and he can stay there whenever he visits us' (2 K 4:10).

OUR HOPES AND EXPECTATIONS

Neither panic nor unconcern
There are fewer priests, and they are getting older. Young priests are becoming rare. These are facts which concern us all, and there is cause for anxiety. Not all the faithful are aware of this: there seem to be plenty of priests around, they say; is there really a problem?

Yes, there is cause for concern – but no reason for panic. There are priests in our area, and there continue to be new candidates to the priesthood. We have deacons, pastoral agents and many lay people helping in parishes, schools, hospitals and movements.

Besides, we should be a little restrained in our concern; after all, other Churches are much more seriously affected by this problem. The lack of priests in some of the younger Churches – and in older ones – has reached much more alarming proportions. To them, our situation seems one of great abundance and luxury. Nor is it the first time in history that our Church has had to manage with fewer priests.

One thing is certain, however: in future, priests will no longer be able to provide all of the services which the people of God have come to expect from us. Even now, it is no longer possible for each parish to have its own priest; nor can a priest be assigned to each hospital, each school, and each movement. It seems likely that this trend will continue. Intensive à la carte pastoral care will no longer be possible everywhere. This does not mean that we have become less available; it simply means that our resources are not what they used to be. This is of course an impoverishment, but it is by no means a catastrophe.

Are there any alternatives?

Now and then, people suggest specific ways in which we might deal with the shortage of priests. It has been suggested that the conditions for admission could be made more flexible, and that celibacy, for example, should no longer be a requirement; perhaps then we would have more candidates. Aside from the fact that the obligation to celibacy was reaffirmed by Vatican II, and confirmed by a later Synod, we must ask ourselves whether this is indeed the main cause of the low number of candidates to the priesthood. The situation in those Churches which do not require celibacy is not promising. In today's climate of generalised eroticism, would the suppression of this requirement be properly understood? Would it truly be a prophetic act?

It is interesting to note that the shortage of candidates to the priesthood is paralleled by an even greater decrease in the number of vocations to the consecrated life, especially among women. We should also note that the third generation of committed laity is somewhat slow in coming forward. Perhaps we should be at least equally concerned – if not more so – about these two parallel developments. Perhaps we should look for the reasons at a deeper level. Would we discover that our faith has become less lively, less alert, less imbued with missionary spirit, and that the fire of charity within us does not burn with the same ardour as it once did? It would not be the first time in history that this has happened. Each time, reformers and saints have appeared to rekindle the flame. This is precisely what is happening in our own time: in some places, we are witnessing a powerful resurgence of the faith, and the radical adhesion to gospel values, which lead to total consecration. There is no shortage of vocations in these places, because there is a new respect for the significance and the intrinsic value of consecrated celibacy.

Other voices have been raised in favour of the admission of women to the priesthood. What should we think of this? Jesus did not admit women to the priesthood. Was this by chance, or perhaps because of the dominant cultural model, which has since changed? There are those who think so. We should note, however, that Jesus acted with great freedom with respect to laws and traditions in other areas of life; he would not have considered them an obstacle had he wanted to break away from custom in this particular area. He did not do so. The great tradition of Christian Churches did not do so either. To support this tradition with rational arguments – to the extent that this is possible – would require an in-depth analysis of the biblical anthropology of men and women, of their specificity and of their partnership according to God's will. Pope John Paul II has provided such an analysis in a theological meditation in his letter *On the dignity and vocation of women* (*Mulieris dignitatem*). It would be impossible to provide even a brief summary of the Pope's meditation in this pastoral letter. Besides, the problem of the priesthood of women is not a problem of the theology of priesthood; it would be more appropriate to discuss it in the context of the theology of men and women and of their places in the plan of God, Creator and Redeemer.

The pastoral ministry of vocations

Be that as it may, the fact remains that we need priests. And our time, as much as any other period in history, is God's time. We must do all we can to foster new vocations to the priesthood. To this end we need an intensive pastoral ministry of vocations.

What does this mean? The expression 'pastoral ministry

of vocations' is in itself rather strange. Can we promote vocations through strategies and marketing systems? A pastoral vocations plan can obviously never be some kind of emergency relief plan; it is rather an expression of the firm belief that God continues to call men to the priesthood, in our time as he did in the past - an expression of the hope that young men can still respond generously to this call. A pastoral plan for promoting vocations can do no more than strengthen God's call – much as John the Baptist did in the desert – and remove the obstacles which might stand in the way of a positive response.

A correct understanding of priesthood

The image of the priest has, of course, evolved over the centuries: the itinerant apostle of the scriptures was not the bishop-prince of the Middle Ages; the priest of the Ancien Régime was not the parish priest we know today. Lifestyles have changed, but the essence of the priest, as it is presented to us in the scriptures and through tradition, has remained unchanged. It is useful to have a sense of history as we try to discern what is unchangeable and what is the result of particular historical circumstances.

If we want to have more priests, it is vital that we define their identity with rigorous precision: they are fully integrated among the people, but they have a mission of their own, one that no one else can assume in their place; their priestly service does not rest on some pragmatic distribution of labour among the people of God. This means that ministerial priesthood is essential, not merely optional, to the life of the Church.

It is quite natural that some young people should hesitate to commit themselves to a function whose claim to necessity rests only on vague and secondary foundations. When we discuss priests and their mission, therefore, we must do so with great care and clarity. The priest proclaims the Word with apostolic guarantee; through the sacraments, he makes present Christ's salvation; he presides over communities with the authority of a pastor and the love of Jesus himself; he assists people in their search for meaning in their lives; he is the eyes through which God sees the suffering of the entire world, and he must help to bear and to heal this suffering. A clear message concerning priesthood is vitally important, for, as St Paul says, 'And if the man who plays the bugle does not sound a clear call, who will prepare for battle?' (1 Co 14:8). If we are to have more vocations, we must first have a clear definition of the priesthood.

Asking for labourers to bring in the harvest

We cannot produce priests; we can only receive them. We cannot control the growth of vocations in the Church; we must ask for priests in our prayers. The gospels teach us that Jesus himself prayed for this in the night. 'The harvest is large, but there are few workers to gather it in. Pray to the owner of the harvest that he will send out workers to gather in his harvest' (Mt 9:37).

Do our communities, our parishes, and our schools really pray sincerely and intensely – on other days besides Vocations Sunday – for an increase in vocations? Or do we pray half-heartedly, all the while believing in our hearts that there are probably other ways around the issue? Are we filled with the 'burning faith that moves mountains' when we pray for vocations?

The rich soil of family life

Vocations are usually born in families where love and self-denial are the fabric of daily life. They are the fruit of the kind of overabundant justice which goes beyond the bare minimum demanded by the Commandments, producing a family life which is in accordance with the new law, the law of the Beatitudes and of the Sermon on the Mount.

Read chapters 5 and 6 of St Matthew's gospel; you will find in them all that is needed for a family to become a rich soil wherein vocations may grow – an environment in which the Beatitudes are taken for granted and provide the guidelines for daily behaviour. Such an environment is poor in spirit, gentle, pure, compassionate and ready to forgive, hungry and thirsty for justice; an environment in which no one is afraid of being criticised or persecuted for being Christian. Above all, in these homes there is prayer, sharing and giving, and hospitality is practised without undue concern for the future, in a spirit of trust that 'our Father in Heaven knows what we need'.

In these homes, the parents – in the secret of their hearts, sometimes unbeknownst to each other – pray and keep their hearts open to the call that God may address to their children.

Loving the Church as she is

Priests are men of the Church. It is right that they should be identified with her. Any criticism of the Church affects them personally; they suffer with her. They know that it is their duty to work constantly for the reform of the Church; for although she is pure, she must be purified continually. However, we cannot reform the Church if we begin with an entirely negative image of her. No priest can survive for long in the schizophrenic position of being both a servant of the Church and a bitter and detached critic. A priest who entrenched himself in such an attitude would quickly fall into depression and ultimately destroy himself. At first, this attitude would merely exhaust him; later it would lead to frustration, and finally to bitterness. As priests, we must love the Church. Our own happiness depends on this.

Moreover, it is difficult for young men to become

priests if they do not live in an environment where the Church is loved. This does not mean that we should deny or conceal the Church's faults, or be silent about them. Many saints have vigorously denounced the Church's hierarchy and its members. But they have always done so with caring. In this year when we celebrate St Bernard, I am reminded of his letter to his confrère Pope Eugene III (*De Consideratione*). I also think of St Catherine of Siena, who wrote her most severe letters to the Pope in Avignon, but who always addressed him as '*il dolce Cristo in terra*' (the gentle Christ on earth). We shall have no vocations unless we can create places where the Church is truly loved.

Entering the Church has always been something of a shock, for old and young alike. Did the first Christians enjoy the thought of risking their lives to join a persecuted Church? Was it any easier at the time of the French Revolution, when priests and religious were put to death by the thousands? Or in the Churches of Eastern Europe, which until recently lived under the cold threat of dictatorships? Was it such an easy choice to become a priest in one of these Churches? By comparison, the shock experienced by young men who enter today is certainly not unbearable. They may often be the only young people present at Eucharistic celebrations presided over by elderly or greying priests, but this does not require a faith tried by fire.

In an environment with a positive attitude towards the Church, young people can gradually learn to make the transition from the Church of their dreams, or the Church that they think they could build with their own hands, to the Church as it is, an object of faith and of grace, the Church which we receive from the hands of God. They can make the transition from a Church which they contemplate to a Church in which they live and work. Those who look at the Church from the outside, as spectators, will react in such terms as 'How beautiful,' or 'How ugly'; 'This is for me,' or 'This does not suit me.' They will pass judgment merely on the basis of subjective emotions, or according to passing moods. Those who enter and take their place in the Church do not pass judgment. They say, 'This is my Church; she gives me life. She is my concern.'

The Church may be old, but she is not ossified. In every age, she has periodically left her quiet garden for the unknown forests of other peoples and cultures, for the land of Naphtali and Zebulon, the Galilee of the Gentiles. Today, she will again find her way into the new cultures of the younger generation. These often do not have a Christian past, a Christian tradition, or Christian memories. But they have been touched by something. They may be in a hurry; they are often impatient; they have a profound dislike for long-winded and roundabout approaches. But God (and the Church) calls them wherever they are, however unprepared and inadequate they may seem. The prophet Amos, describing his own call, said, 'I am not the kind of prophet who prophesies for pay. I am a herdsman and I take care of fig-trees. But the Lord took me from my work as a shepherd and ordered me to come and prophesy to his people' (Am 7:14-15). God will do the same for the Amoses of our time.

Through your demands we become more fully priests
Priests are shaped by the demands and expectations of their brothers and sisters in faith. You help us greatly when you demand that we give you what we, as priests, are able to and want to give.

Ask us, then, to be truly men of God. Demand that we listen more attentively to the gospel, that we devote ourselves more assiduously to prayer, to worship, to praise, to intercession. Ask us to seek holiness incessantly; to proclaim the gospel faithfully, omitting nothing and falsifying nothing, making no concessions but always mindful of your daily problems. Ask us for the sacraments, especially for the Eucharist and the Sacrament of Reconciliation. Demand that our hearts be in harmony with all that is good and beautiful, but also with pain and suffering. Ask us not to remain aloof - rather to become involved in justice, peace and liberation. Ask us, as missionaries and evangelisers, to step beyond the intimate circle of those who share our faith. Demand from us all those things which in your hearts you know to be the things for which priests are called and ordained. You yourselves know what a priest must be and what he must do. Nobody needs to teach you this; in this too St John's words are confirmed: 'As long as his spirit remains in you, you do not need anyone to teach you' (1 Jn 2:27).

The primary mission of the laity

How can you help us? Perhaps you have spontaneously thought of ways in which you can be of assistance within the Church, in liturgies, in catechesis, or in other works which contribute to the growth of your communities.

You are very welcome to help us in this work within the Church. But you can do more. Many of the faithful believe that it is only by working within the Church that they can truly cooperate in the work of building up the Kingdom of God. This is not so. The Kingdom of God grows primarily outside the Church, in the field, amongst the people, in the world. You can help us most by making Christ's Spirit present in your home, in your work, in your profession, in the worlds of economics and politics, in culture, in schools, in health care institutions. All of this is true cooperation in the task of building up the

Church. And this is your specific task; it is the authentic secular apostolate in the middle of the *saeculum* – the world. To be present in the world and in life, and to discern therein what is in conformity with the gospel, and to bear witness to it: all this is not merely a prelude to the coming of the Kingdom of God. It is the Kingdom itself, already established and founded. This is the greatest help you can give us. And here no priest, as a priest, can replace you. And no work within the Church can ever serve as an alibi justifying neglect of the secular apostolate.

Helping within the Church

After this secular apostolate, there are those tasks within the Church which, especially in our times, have been entrusted to you, and in which we welcome and value your assistance.

Countless lay people lend us a helping hand in thousands of material tasks; these include maintenance of church buildings and premises, transport, administrative work, accounting, and the entire infrastructure of those services which are essential to the life of a community of believers. As time goes on, we shall become increasingly dependent on you for much of this work, and we are very grateful for your help.

Thousands of you participate even more directly, as leaders and animators of the Christian community –- in parish teams and councils, in choirs and liturgical groups, in preparation for baptism, confirmation, communion and marriage, in religious instruction, in ministry to the sick, in movements and in schools. The seeds have sprouted and grown over the past twenty years, and they are bearing abundant fruit.

Some lay people have undertaken long-term in-depth formation programmes and have invested considerable time and money in this process. We rejoice in this and we would like to reward these sacrifices – in every sense of the word. Unfortunately, our resources are limited, but the will is there.

If all of these efforts are to grow in harmony with the work of deacons and of priests, we obviously need some form of flexible coordination. We all have a great deal to learn in this respect. We priests are sometimes too slow, too distrustful, too anxious; we lack trust and courage. After all, we are only human.

The Second Vatican Council told us: 'Priests should be willing to listen to lay people, give brotherly consideration to their wishes, and recognise their experience and competence in the different fields of human activity. In this way they will be able to recognise with them the signs of the times... Priests should also be confident in giving lay people charge of duties in the service of the Church, giving them freedom and opportunity for activity and even inviting them, when opportunity occurs, to take the initiative in undertaking projects of their own.' (*Decree on the Ministry and Life of Priests*, 9)

With a few rare exceptions, we priests try to put these recommendations into practice. We sincerely wish to recognise and to promote your responsibilities.

However, we ask you, in turn, to recognise our own specificity, in a spirit of trust. The same document also states: 'For the exercise of this ministry, as for the rest of the priests' functions, a spiritual power is given them, a power whose purpose is to build up... the Church' (ibid. 6).

No doubt it is legitimate to discuss the manner in which a priest exercises this spiritual power. It is possible to comment on this to the priest, and even to criticise him. 'Fraternal correction,' which is mentioned in the gospels, must surely apply to him. But while the manner in which the priest exercises his authority is open to criticism, the fact that 'Priests exercise the function of Christ

as Pastor and Head in proportion to their share of authority… in the name of the bishop' (ibid., 6) is not.

Celibate 'for the sake of the Kingdom'

Priests remain celibate. This is not always understood in
our times, even among Christians. The question 'Why
shouldn't a priest marry?' almost invariably arises in meet-
ings with young people.

Some arguments for celibacy are partly correct, but
ultimately inadequate. For example, it is sometimes said
that priests do not marry because celibacy increases their
capacity for work, allowing them to work harder and better in the service of the Church. This is certainly true, but
is it really a valid argument? Many married people work
very hard indeed. And after all, the Church is not a
Japanese enterprise, where all must be sacrificed to productivity.

No rational arguments can fully explain celibacy 'for
the sake of the Kingdom'. It is a matter of love, and love
cannot be explained in rational terms. Jesus said, 'This
teaching does not apply to everyone, but only to those to
whom God has given it… let him who can accept this
teaching do so' (Mt 19:11-12). Celibacy is founded on a
love that is unique in that it seeks its path in an exclusive
imitation of Christ, in total consecration to him; and this
consecration is linked, according to Christ himself (see
Mt 19:29), to a very special kind of fruitfulness. Priests
remain celibate above all not for the sake of efficiency, or
to increase their productivity, or to have more available
time, but out of love for and faith in Christ, whom they
want to follow closely. In addition, celibacy is a concrete
witness to the conviction that all created values are rela-
tive: God alone is first and absolute. The economy of
redemption is superior to that of creation.

To live unmarried for the sake of the Kingdom of God

is also a profession of vigorous faith in eschatological realities and in eternal life. The difficulties people experience in understanding and appreciating priestly celibacy are not due merely to the current attitudes which have made absolute values of sexuality and eroticism; these difficulties are also due to our society's waning faith in immortality, the after-life and resurrection.

If we believe that to die is to disappear, then to die childless is indeed a cruel fate. Nothing would be left of us – not even a child! Our deepest impulse, the desire to live forever, cannot accept this. Thus the absence – or the weakening – of belief in immortality is always associated with difficulties in understanding the place of virginity. The Old Testament, written in times when immortality was only vaguely understood and was seen as a twilight existence in a world of shadows, could not accept the idea of remaining unmarried. It is noteworthy that St Augustine, in defining virginity, did not even mention marriage or sexuality; for him, it is entirely linked to the concept of immortality: 'Virginity is a constant meditation on immortality, even while we still live in mortal bodies.'

Celibacy becomes very difficult for us when sensitivity to gospel and Church teachings, on purity in general and conjugal morality in particular, is weakened among the faithful. On this point, the Church is almost in opposition to a certain kind of modern mentality. If the faithful speak up only faintly, or not at all, in debates on this issue, it will become increasingly difficult for priests to choose celibacy joyfully.

How do we react when we see sexual pleasure turned into some kind of absolute right? Surely this is elevating a created reality to the rank of a false god or idol. Do we have the courage to oppose this kind of deification as irreconcilable with the worship of the one true God? It is particularly difficult for a priest to live a celibate life if he is alone in an environment where eroticism and sex are made into absolute values.

Do we ever, in the course of conversation, dare to take the side of those who choose celibacy for the sake of the Kingdom – be they priests, religious or lay? And what happens when one of our own children chooses this path? Many Christians want faithful and celibate priests and religious; but their admiration and their desire remain somewhat platonic. Recently, a religious community was obliged to close one of its houses in a low-income neighbourhood. As soon as this became known, an angry woman attacked the mother superior: 'You cannot do this! You are taking our sisters away!' 'We have no more vocations,' answered the mother superior, and added, 'If your daughter wished to become a religious, would you let her?' The woman's response was a spontaneous 'No!'; she wanted grandchildren, she said.

Towards a Church with fewer resources

We must look for a solution to the problem of the dwindling number of priests in our part of the world. No doubt we shall have to explore different paths: regrouping parishes and streamlining pastoral activities; setting clear priorities, since we can no longer do everything; redistributing available resources; involving lay people even in specifically ecclesial tasks.

But we must be honest: the problem will not be solved merely through efficient reorganisation and reconversion. Something more will have to be done. To begin with, we must accept, joyfully and serenely, the knowledge that, as a Church, we are becoming increasingly poor. This is true in financial terms, in terms of staffing, in terms of our impact on public life and the media, and perhaps also in terms of our intellectual potential and the competence and academic training of our leaders. There is no doubt that we are becoming poorer in numbers!

But here is our hope: a poorer Church is not necessarily impoverished in the quality of its love and devotion to God and to humanity. Poverty can even enrich us: it can free us from a 'rich' and self-sufficient conception of pastoral ministry, renewal and new evangelisation. What is important is not what we plan for tomorrow, but rather God's dream for his Church at the end of this millennium. Clearly, his ways are not our ways. Probably the big projects we envision are not what is needed; what is important is what God gives us to share. Perhaps this poverty will make priests more aware of the essential values of our priesthood: the mystery of our vocation; the power of our ordination and of our mission; faith in the irresistible power of the gospel proclaimed in all its purity, without rhetorical and artificial embellishments; faith in the quiet power of the sacraments; the prestige of a more spiritual authority.

This happened to the children of Israel. Every time their external supports – the king, the temple, their land – weakened or disappeared, Israel's faith deepened and the people grew closer to God. Was it not precisely during and after the time of exile that psalmists and prophets wrote their most moving texts?

Poverty is as old as the Church itself. It is congenital. The story of Jesus began in Bethlehem, after all, and led to Calvary. The manger and the cross have remained at the heart of the Church to this day. Poverty did not prevent the shepherds and the magi from coming to see Christ. And no sooner did Jesus die on the Cross than 'he gathered all things to himself': the centurion, the fearful notables Nicodemus and Joseph. If a grain of wheat dies, 'it produces many grains' (Jn 12:24).

Is this merely a way of consoling ourselves, or an

attempt to make a virtue of necessity? No. This is the naked truth of the gospels: only a faith that is poor can be solid ground on which to stand. No other supports will sustain us through the cold winters of this world. There is no alternative. Poverty will not take our joy from us; it will increase it. We priests are ready to contribute to this joy (see 2 Co 1:20). We want to be messengers of joy!